Dad's fun run

Dad is on a run to get fit.

Dad runs and hums.

A bug hops on Dad's lip.

Dad taps at the bug.

Dad runs into lots of mud.

Dad hits his leg on a log.

Dad gets on the bus.

Dad's fun run

Level 2, Set 2: Story 19

Before reading

Say the sounds: g o b h e r f u l

Practise blending the sounds: Dad's fun run get fit runs Dad hums bug hops lip taps lots mud hits leg log gets bus

High-frequency words: on a at it not
Tricky words: is to the into of his no
Vocabulary check: hums – sings without words

Story discussion: Where is Dad on the cover picture? Do you think he's having fun?

Teaching points: Check that children can say the phonemes /g/ /o/ /b/ /h/ /e/ /r/ /f/ /u/ /l/, and that they can identify the grapheme that goes with each phoneme.
Check that they can read with expression, taking account of punctuation, especially full stops and exclamation marks.
Check that children can identify and read the tricky words: is, to, the, into, of, his, no.

After reading

Comprehension:
- How is Dad feeling at the start of the story?
- What hops on to Dad's lip?
- Why does Dad have to stop running?
- Is Dad happy at the end of the story? How do you know?

Fluency: Speed-read the words again from the inside front cover.